SECOND GRADE
LEARNING MATHEMATICS FROM PICTURES TO WORDS

AUTHORS

DR. EDWARD C. HAYNIE

LAMAR HART

Table of Contents

Acknowledgements

This booklet is dedicated to Dr. Joyce Taylor Haynie for her interest, support, and belief in STEM (Science, Technology, Engineering, and Mathematics) and to Ethan Haynie who strongly encouraged the writing of this booklet. He believed that having strong skills in mathematics helped propel his career success in the field of Architecture.

Great appreciation is extended to Edward C. Haynie, Jr. for his marketing skills and to Jibri Robinson in recognition of his artistic skills in preparation of this booklet. Captain Patrick R. Haynie has been an inspiration while serving as an officer in the U.S. Marines.

Overview

This booklet presents a way for scholars to learn mathematical words from pictures. Word development is fundamentally used to improve reading, writing, mathematics, and science skills. We encourage all parents and teachers to emphasize learning in these areas for their young scholars. The pictures represent mathematical words that students need to know and understand to prepare for reading and completing word problems.

Goals for Mathematics in Second Grade
- Enhance students' knowledge, understanding and skills related to Mathematics sight words.
- Help children to develop mathematic reasoning, skills, and enhance their ability to solve practical problems.
- Contribute to children's conceptual understanding of the world around them.
- Foster the development of positive attitudes in studying Mathematics.

Second Grade
How Children Learn Mathematics From Pictures to Words.

Children learn Mathematics concepts from both the informal, unstructured experiments in their environment and the more formal, structured educational setting known as school.

The objectives of this booklet are to assist teachers to understand how children learn basic mathematics skills and solve problems.

Learning Theories Applied to Mathematics for Second Grade:

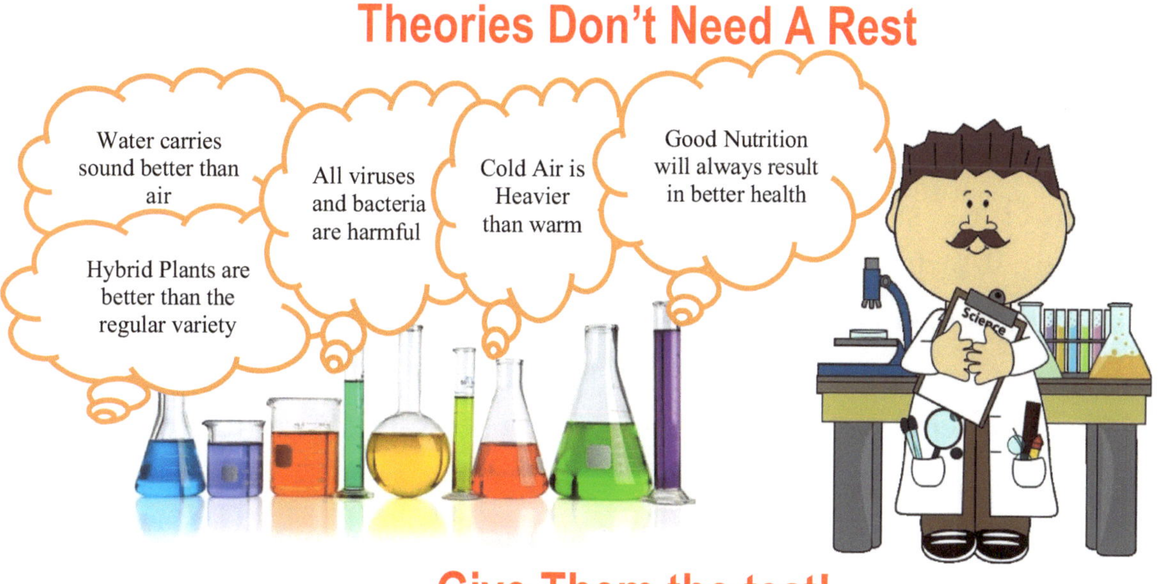

The Constructivists/Cognitive (Learning in action)
- Constructivists believe that children must be allowed to experiment physically with the things around them if they are to learn. They believe active learning builds mental structures.
- Jean Piaget:
  - Theory is age and stage related, which means that students go through definite developmental stages in their lives. Each stage must be completed before a person can attain the next stage.
  - Concrete Operations Stage (6 years old – 12 years old) Action on Operations
    - Children will "operate" on objects by systematically filling containers back and forth; they will make statements that acknowledge the interrelatedness of the objects; will show that they understand how to reverse actions by filling and unfilling containers.

Second Grade

The aim in Learning Mathematics From Pictures to Words is to build mathematics skills for Second Grade students.
- Functions of Words
  - Read the word and draw a picture
- Basic Expressions
  - Dialogue with the correct pictures and complete a sentence.
- Making Short Sentences
  - Complete the sentences with the words from the pictures.

Second Grade Common Core Standards

The Second Grade common core standards provide students with a firm foundation while learning whole numbers, addition, subtraction, and multiplication. As students progress, these standards prepare them for enhanced for learning and application of more demanding mathematics concepts and procedures.

Research supports the recommendation that efforts to enhance knowledge and skills in mathematics for Second Grade should focus on the number core; learning how numbers correspond to quantities, and learning how to put numbers together and to take them apart (the beginning of addition and subtraction). These are complicated ideas that take time to learn. Research also suggests that without these critical building blocks in place, mathematics performance will suffer in later grades.

Operations and Algebraic Thinking

- Represent and solve problems involving addition and subtraction.
- Add and subtract within 20.
- Work with equal groups of objects to gain foundations for multiplication.

Number and Operations in Base Ten

- Understand place value.
- Use place value understanding and properties of operations to add and subtract.

Measurement and Data

- Measure and estimate lengths in standard units.
- Relate addition and subtraction to length.
- Work with time and money.
- Represent and interpret data.

Geometry

- Reason with shapes and their attributes.

- Make sense of problems and persevere in solving them.
- Reason abstractly and quantitatively.
- Construct viable arguments and critique the reasoning of others.
- Model with mathematics.
- Use appropriate tools strategically.
- Attend toprecision.
- Look for and make use of structure.
- Look for and express regularity in repeated reasoning.

Words to Know

1. Add
2. Addition sentence
3. After
4. Angle
5. Array
6. Bar graph
7. Before
8. Cent
9. Centimeter
10. Coins
11. Column
12. Compare
13. Data
14. Decimal point
15. Digits
16. Dime
17. Dollar
18. Dollar sign
19. Doubles
20. Edge
21. Equal
22. Estimate
23. Even
24. Expanded form
25. Face
26. Flat surface
27. Foot
28. Fourths
29. Greater than
30. Greatest value
31. Half dollar
32. Half past
33. Halves
34. Height
35. Hexagon
36. Hour
37. Hundred
38. Inch (in.)
39. Join
40. Length
41. Less than
42. Line plot
43. Mental math
44. Meter (m.)
45. Minute
46. Near doubles
47. Nickel
48. Number line
49. Number sentence
50. Number word
51. Odd
52. Order
53. Parallelogram
54. Part
55. Penny
56. Pentagon
57. Pictograph
58. Plane shape
59. Polygon
60. Pyramid
61. Quadrilateral
62. Quarter
63. Quarter past
64. Quarter to
65. Regroup
66. Related
67. Row
68. Separate
69. Side
70. Solid figures
71. Standard form
72. Subtract
73. Subtraction sentence
74. Tally mark
75. Thirds
76. Thousand
77. Trapezoid
78. Unequal
79. Unit
80. Vertex
81. Whole
82. Width
83. Yard

Learning Mathematics from Pictures to Words

1. add

When you add, you join groups together.

$$2+3=5$$

2. addition sentence

$$5+3=8$$

3. after

12 comes after 11

$$12-11$$

4. angle

An angle is when two lines meet at the vertex.

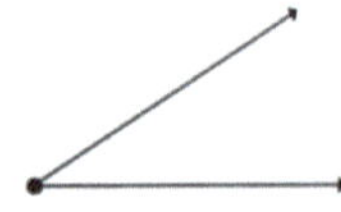

5. array

An array shows the same number of things in each row.

$$4+4+8=12$$

6. bar graph

A bar graph uses bars to show data.

7. before

8 comes before 9

$$8-9$$

8. cent

9. centimeter (cm.)

A centimeter is a metric unit used to measure length.

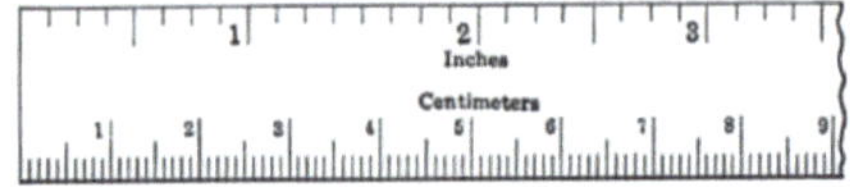

10. coins

11. column

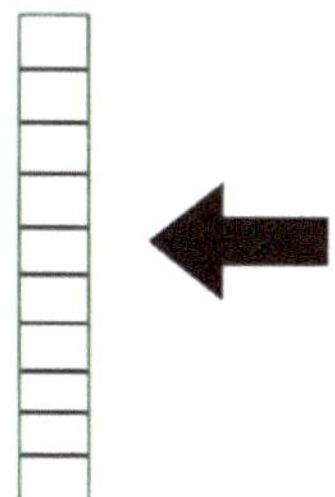

16. dime

12. compare

When you compare numbers, you find out if a number is greater than, less than, or equal to a number.

122 > 65

17. dollar

13. data

18. dollar sign

The dollar sign is the symbol that is placed before the numbers when you are writing an amount of money.

$

14. decimal point

A decimal point separates dollars from cents.

0.5

19. doubles

A doubles fact has two addends that are the same.

$2+2=4$

15. digits

Numbers have 1 or more digits

67 has 2 digits.   0 1 2 3 4 5 6 7 8 9

20. edge

An edge is where two flat surfaces of a solid figure meet.

21. equal

Equal means to have the same amount, size, number, or value.

26. flat surface

22. estimate

When you make an estimate, you make a good guess.

27. foot (ft)

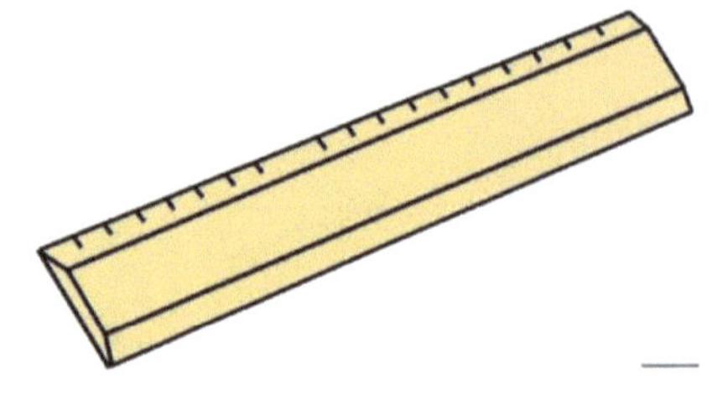

23. even

An even number can be shown as two equal parts.

2,4,6,8,10

28. fourths

When 1 whole is separated into 4 equal parts, the parts are called fourths.

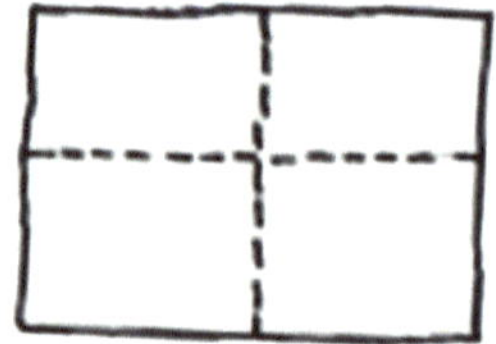

24. expanded form

Expanded form shows the place value of each digit.

$30+5+15+3=53$

29. greater than

11 is greater than 10

11 10

25. face

The flat surface of a solid that does not roll is called a face.

30. greatest value

The coin that has the greatest value is the one that is worth the most.

31. half dollar

36. hour

An hour is 60 minutes.

32. half past

Half past is 30 minutes past the hour.

37. hundred

10 tens make 1 hundred.

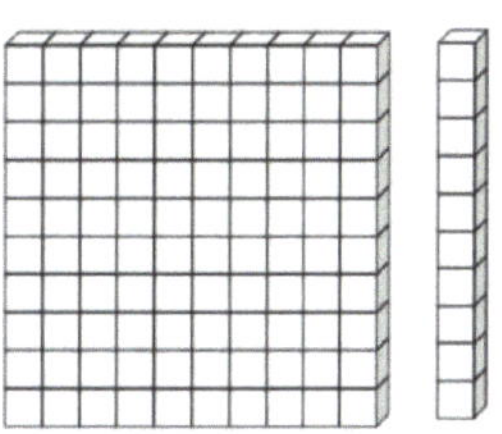

33. halves

When 1 whole is separated into 2 equal parts, the parts are called halves.

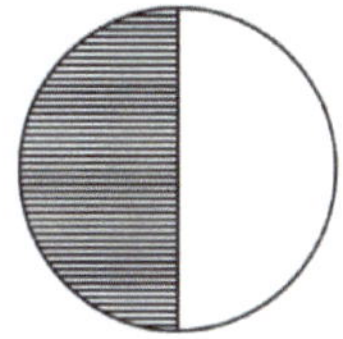

38. inch (in.)

An inch is a standard unit used to measure length.

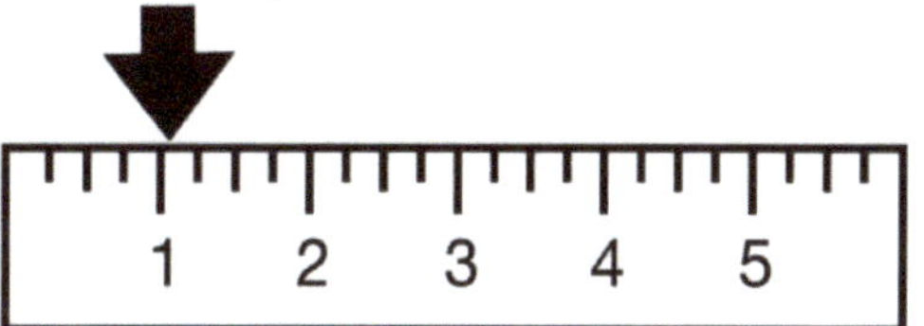

34. height

Height is how tall something is.

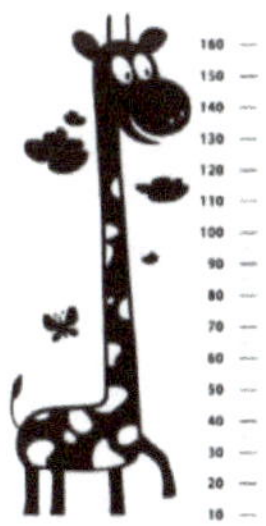

39. join

To join means to put together.

35. hexagon

A hexagon is a plane that has 6 sides.

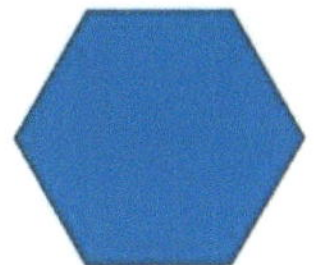

40. length

Length is the distance from one end of an object to the other end.

41. less than

8 is less than 15

42. line plot

A way to organize data on a number line.

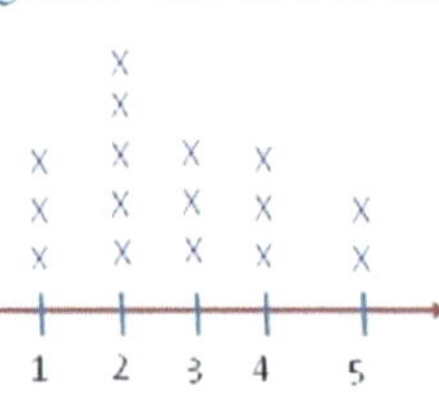

43. mental math

Mental math is math you do in your head.

44. meter (m)

45. minute

There are 60 minutes in 1 hour.

46. near doubles

An addition fact with near doubles has an addend that is one more than the other addend.

$$3 + 4 = 7$$

47. nickel

48. number line

A number line is a line that shows numbers in order from left to right.

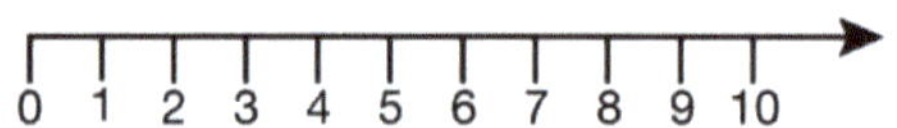

49. number sentence

A number sentence has an operation symbol (+ or -) and an equal sign (=).

$$7+9=16$$

50. number word

A number word uses words. The number word for 45 is forty-five.

$$45-0=45$$

51. odd

An odd number cannot be divided into two equal parts.

3, 5, 7, 9

52. order

Numbers can be put in counting order from least to greatest or from greatest to least.

53. parallelogram

A parallelogram is a plane that has 4 sides. The opposite sides are parallel.

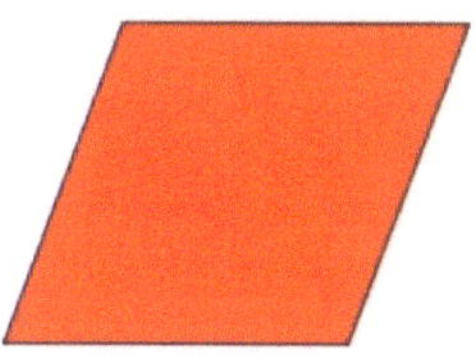

54. part

A part is a piece of a whole.

55. penny

56. pentagon

A pentagon is a plane shape with five sides, vertices, and five angles.

57. pictograph

A pictograph uses pictures to show data.

58. plane shape

A plane shape is a flat shape.

59. polygon

A polygon is a plane shape with 3 or more sides.

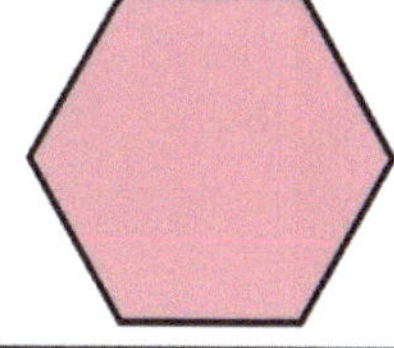

60. pyramid

A pyramid is a solid figure.

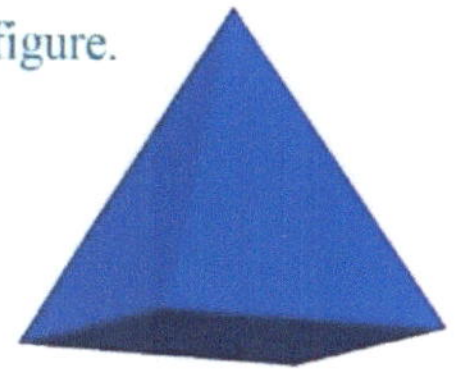

61. quadrilateral

A quadrilateral is a polygon with four sides.

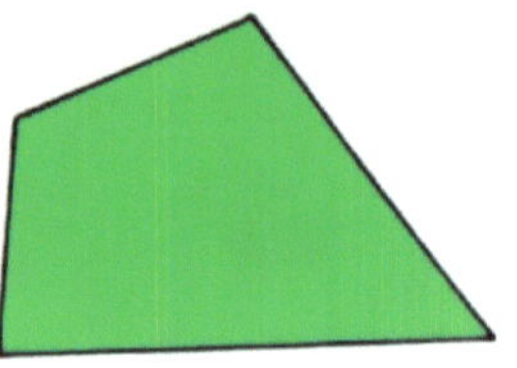

62. quarter

63. quarter past

15 minutes after the hour.

64. quarter to

15 minutes before the hour.

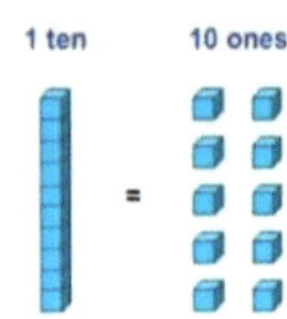

65. regroup

10 ones can be regrouped to make 1 ten.

66. related

Addition facts and subtraction facts are related if they have the same numbers.

$$2+5=7$$
$$7-2=5$$

67. row

68. separate

To separate can mean to subtract, or to take something apart into two or more parts.

$$8-3=11$$

69. side

A side is a line segment that makes one part of a plane shape.

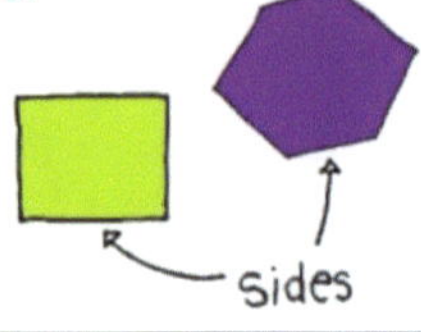

70. solid figures

Solid figures have length, width, and height.

71. standard form

The standard form is a way to write a number using only digits.

2020

76. thousand

10 hundred is equal to 1 thousand

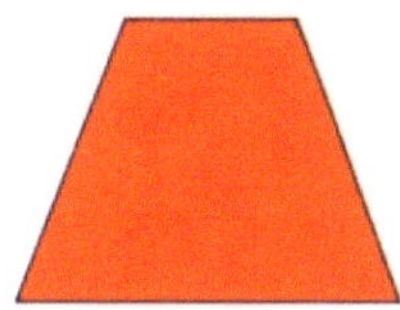

72. subtract

When you subtract, you find out how many are left, or which group has more.

7 - 4 = 3

77. trapezoid

A trapezoid is a plane shape with 4 sides, 4 angles, and 4 vertices.

73. subtraction sentence

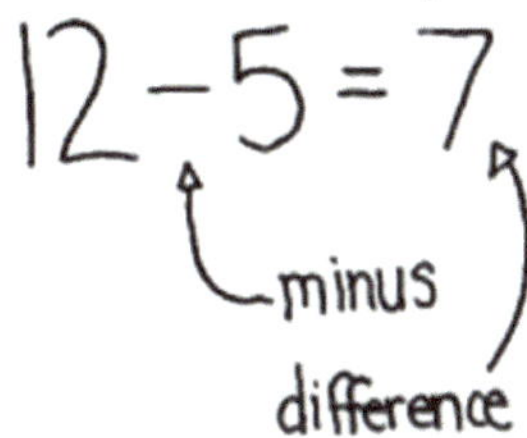

78. unequal

Unequal parts are parts that are not equal.

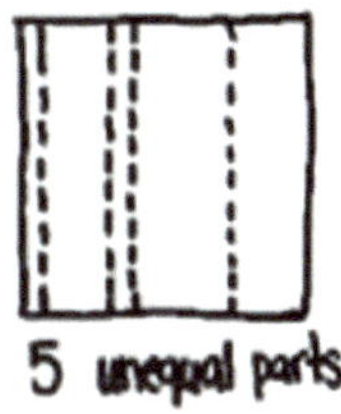

74. tally mark

We use tally marks to keep track of information on an organized list.

79. unit

An inch is a unit that can be used to measure the length of an object.

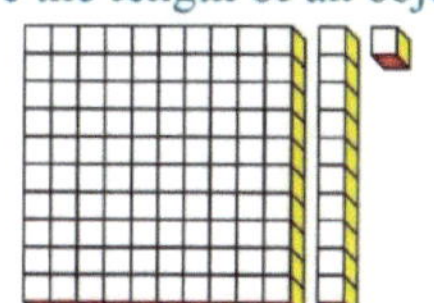

75. thirds

When 1 whole is separated into 3 equal parts, the parts are called thirds.

80. vertex

A vertex is a point where 2 sides or 3 or more edges meet.

81. whole

You can add parts to find the whole.

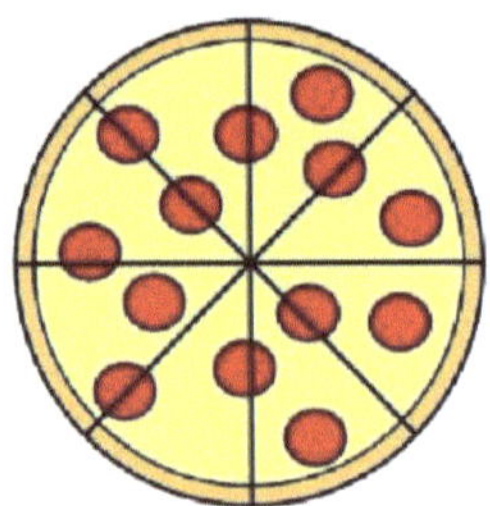

82. width

Width is the distance across an object.

83. yard

A baseball is about a yard long.

Blank Word Cards

The following pages have the pictures without the words. Use them to assess your scholar's knowledge of the sight words.

Suggested use:

- Print out the cards and use them as flash cards.

- Ask the scholar to identify what word(s) are represented by the picture.

2+3=5	
5+3=8	8-9
12-11	
4+4+8=12	

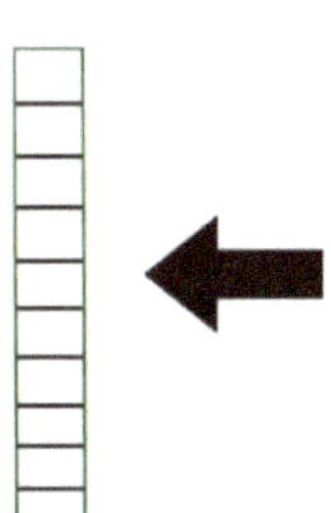

122 > 65

$

0.5

2+2=4

0 1 2 3 4
5 6 7 8 9

9 + 10
is about 20
2,4,6,8,10
30+5+15+3=53
11 10

8 < 15
3 + 4 = 7
15x5=?
0 1 2 3 4 5 6 7 8 9 10
7+9=16
45-0=45
1 HOUR

3,5,7,9

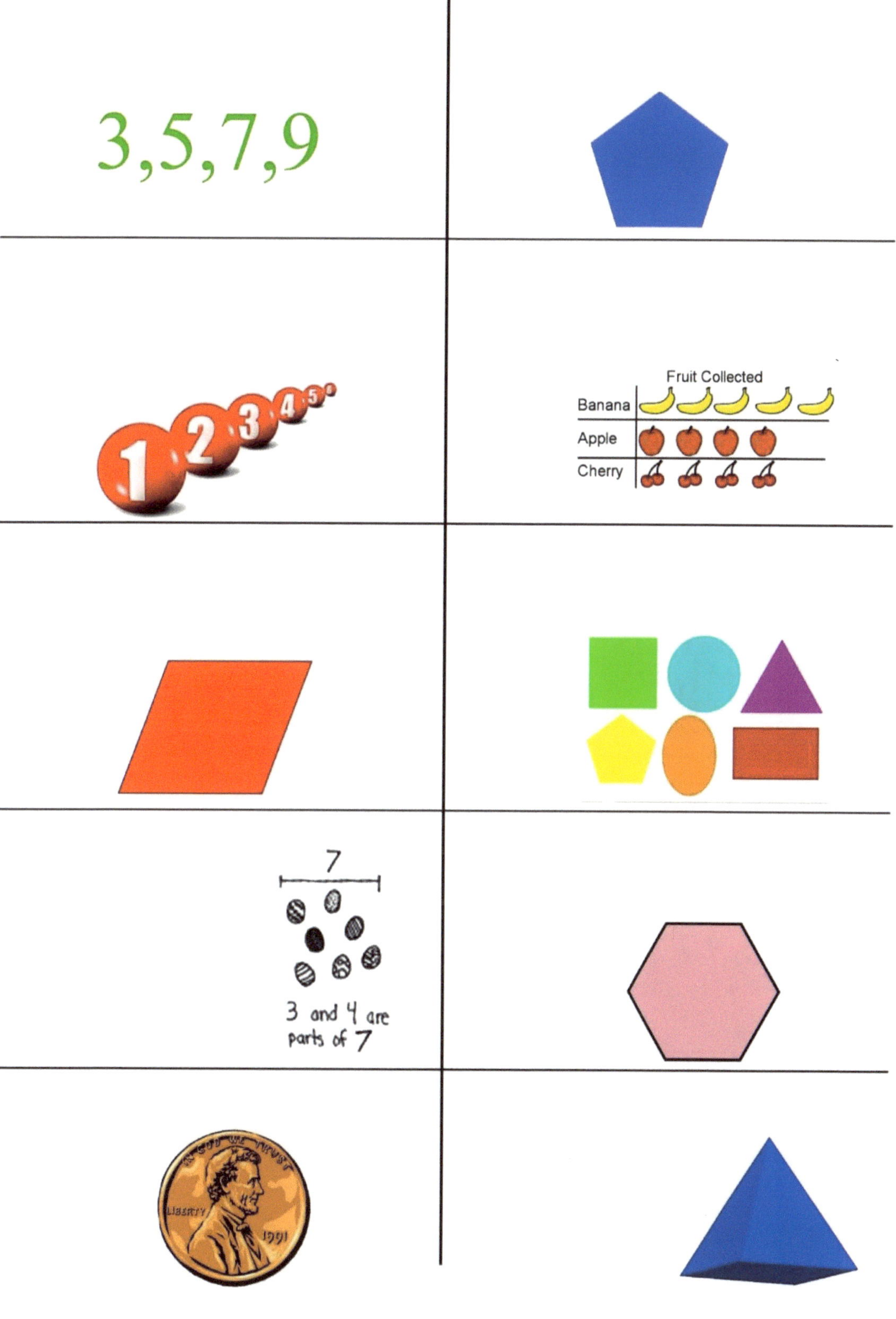

2+5=7
7-2=5
1 2 3 4
11 12 13 14
21 22 23 24
31 32 33 34
row
8-3=11
sides
1 ten   10 ones
=

2020

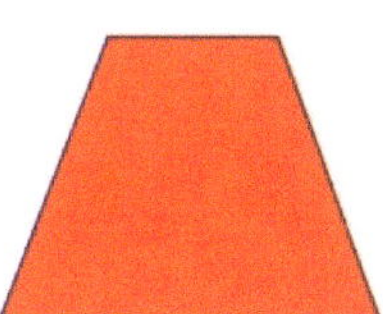

7-4=3

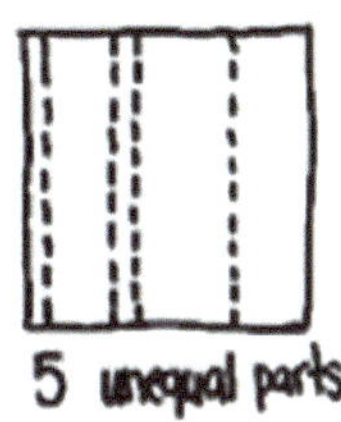

$12 - 5 = 7$

minus

difference

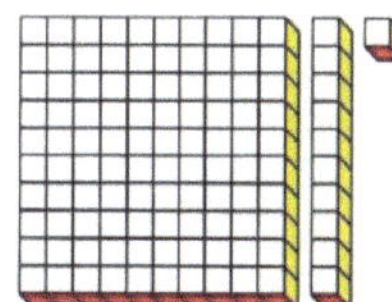

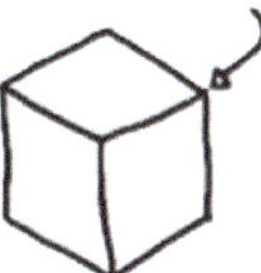

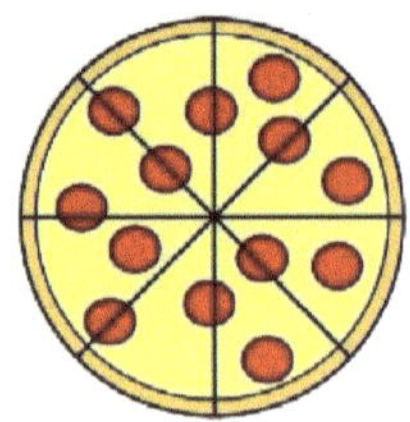

About the Authors

Dr. Edward C. Haynie holds a Bachelor of Science Degree in Chemistry and Mathematics, a Master of Science Degree in Chemistry, and a Doctor of Education Degree in Curriculum and Instruction/Science Education. Haynie has a vast and diverse background in science, which includes experiences in administration, teaching, research, planning, curriculum design and implementation of program in secondary schools, community college and university levels. He is also the Executive Director of the Incubator Scientists Program.

Lamar Hart received his Bachelor of Arts Degree in Computer Science with a minor in mathematics from Saint Louis University. He is a current student at Grand Canyon University, where he is finishing his Master of Education Degree in Early Childhood Education. He has worked in the field of education for over fifteen years as an Information Technology Director and Computer Science teacher, a teacher assistant at Barack Obama Elementary School. He has also worked with Dr. Haynie with the Incubator Scientist Program for the past ten years.

www.ingramcontent.com/pod-product-compliance
Lightning Source LLC
Chambersburg PA
CBHW042124110726
48006CB00003B/755